REVERING

REMINISCING

RECORDANDO

Bilingual Muses of a Centenarian

By Santa Pi

authorHOUSE®

AuthorHouse™
1663 Liberty Drive
Bloomington, IN 47403
www.authorhouse.com
Phone: 1-800-839-8640

First published by AuthorHouse 10/26/2009

ISBN: 978-1-4490-2788-9 (e)
ISBN: 978-1-4490-2785-8 (sc)
ISBN: 978-1-4490-2787-2 (hc)

Library of Congress Control Number: 2009909400

Printed in the United States of America
Bloomington, Indiana

This book is printed on acid-free paper.

DEDICATION

To my daughters, "Nanita" and "Puchi", who have lovingly kept my "poesías" close to heart, and who have safely guarded and compiled them for publication.

Thank you for your love and devoted care.

love, Mami

TABLE OF CONTENTS

TABLA DE CONTENIDO

PART III

PROLOGUE

My life's sojourn with its essence of my life experiences, emotions and thoughts has been captured on the following pages of this three-part book; each part shedding light on the clearly defined epochs of my long-lived life.

Revering: The last few decades has brought me renewed spiritual strength with an intensified recognition of a loving Creator and a mounting desire to praise him with my, Oh, so inadequate words.

Reminiscing: My desperate need to express my loneliness and despair in verse is balanced in my person and on paper by recalling the seemingly unending happy family days surrounded by love and warmth.

Recordando: The book's last part comprises of poems in Spanish about the first part of my life. My loneliness and affirmations expressed in those verses lament the separation from my parents, from my homeland and my idyllic childhood.

I have written simply and honestly and I can only hope that one of my poems will give voice to the reader's deepest sentiment and yearnings.

INTRODUCTION

Abuelita Santa, my grandmother, frequently talks about how she was inspired to love prose. Explaining her motivation she wrote, *"Quite a few decades ago, in a small village by the side of the sea, there lived a little old lady, kind and loving, who gathered together the children of her neighbors at the dusk of evenings to transport them to the most desirable places in the world. I believe she was endowed by a superior power. A power to make the children happy, to make them laugh, to make them dream and to make them wish to be brave heroes or create empires. The little, old lady was very poor in worldly goods, but she was rich with the magical power of proper words, words capable of calming the children's anxieties, their longings, their pain and hunger... The little old lady's stories sweetened the existence of many children, including mine. And although I was the youngest, I never fell asleep. I always listened until the end. The little old lady blessed me every night before I went to sleep. She was my wonderful mother. The stories I heard from her lips have not been forgotten. They were put away like a treasure in a chest."*

Through her adult years, Abuelita would tell us, her grandchildren, the stories she heard as a child...enchanting stories. But most of all, I recall *the way* she told those stories. She had a certain dramatic flair in telling those stories. I later learned that during her youth she had been sought out to give poetic orations at the local theater, frequently mentioning *El Teatro, La Perla,* a grand theatre in Ponce where she would entertain the audience with her dramatic poem recitations.

It was a wonderful moment to celebrate with her the place that had held such fond childhood memories, recalling her provincial beginnings and reminiscing how her passion of verse had given her solace these 100 years.

It was 75 years ago when Abuelita Santa made a difficult decision to leave her familiar Playa de Ponce, Puerto Rico, arriving by ship at New York's harbor on a cold and foggy March morning for a better life than the one she was leaving behind. This poetess' fortitude paved the way for her offspring to have opportunities not afforded her. In "Loving You" she writes,

> *"No matter what old age may bring*
> *The thought of you all in Almighty's hands*
> *Have made dreams come true for me*
> *While abiding in this our blessed land."*

Her love for family and confidence in God's guidance and protection have inspired us all to go beyond our own perceived limitations and reach within the limitless depths of God-given creativity and God-bestowed strength.

Abuelita Santa's memoirs recalling her struggle to earn a living and learn a new language while raising a family alone during the depression years of the 1930s and 1940s, are documented with the Puerto Rican Studies Department at Hunter College, New York.

Her novel published in 2006 entitled, *"Out of Guts, A Heart"* details the life of three Hispanic women economically struggling to live in the Bronx and working together toward a wonderful and productive future.

Santa is the recipient of **The Outstanding Achievement in Poetry Award** (2005) from the International Society of Poets, and selected poems are published in the **International Who's Who in Poetry** (2004, 2005).

It is my sincere hope that you, the reader, will find the poems ("poesías" as Abuelita calls them) inspiring...sweetening your existence, as they have mine.

Virginia Santa
Eldest Grandchild

After 75 years, 100 year old Santa returns to
El Teatro, La Perla, Ponce, Puerto Rico
December 2008
Photo Credit: Dean Knudsen

PART 1

REVERING

I was born in 1908 on the beautiful island of Puerto Rico. My parents gave me a love for verse and literature very early in my life. A resounding voice, a dramatic flair and a love for prose and poetry made me very popular for giving recitations in the late twenties and early thirties when declamation was a desirable way of entertainment.

The following years found me in New York City - homesick and heart broken - when in my native language of Spanish I began writing poetry to ease my pain.

The retirement years have brought me serenity and time to admire the Creator's world which I have expressed in many of my English poems.

One of the poems, "Another Thought", on the surface describes a typical morning in Florida of sunny skies with a brief rain cloud misting the air. Yet to me it reveals that, even in my present peaceful state and deep reverence for the Supreme Being, I still have sad memories which bring me to tears.

HOW GREAT

This morning the mighty sky
Was dressed in almost royal blue
The wind quietly passing by
Was soft and cool;
As I looked up around
Still awed at the mystery above earth
I saw clouds like angels in white satin gowns
With wreaths of pearls upon their heads
I, with my small mind and eyes
And my inherent faith
Could see beyond the mighty space
How great thou art! Oh Lord, I cried.

HOW SHALL I SING?

I want to sing of happiness, but my harp is
mute
I cannot sing of things that I do not know
I can only sing of things that I have seen
Or of things that are within me
Which are things of sorrows.

I shall sing of pain, of parting, of absences
Of solitude, hunger and poverty,
Of anxieties, doubts and insecurities
O the hopelessness and loneliness.

But the greatest sorrows of this world
I can also sing about, for I have seen
The carelessness, the unfaithfulness,
The ungratefulness and thoughtlessness.
And above all, the selfishness and ungodliness.

But I can also sing to GOD
And thank Him, and praise Him
Because though He has given me pain and
sorrow,
He has also given me patience,
Understanding and fortitude.

I can also sing about GOD's love
For those who are lonely, sad and in pain.
And for those who are lost
In their own despair.
Those who cannot love, He loves
And those who can not help themselves
Or are too young, He also loves.

I shall sing to GOD, again and again
For the marvels of this world
For my miracle of faith
That lives forever in my heart.

On my 96th year:

MY BIRTHDAY SONG

Above the green branches of back yard trees
Where it is always Spring
And where the birds come to nest and sing.
I can see the golden sun
Through the rich lace like embroidered pattern
Of dancing leaves
Brightening my day like a grandiose feast.

Then I want to sing and sing and rock
On my rocking chair back and forth
And forget the sorrows,
The age and lonely life.
The Lord, I thanked
With all my heart and mind.

MY FRIEND

I have a wonderful friend
Who brings me joy
With the wonder of His Spring
And touches me with the gentle breath
Of the caressing zephyr;
And who delights me
With a thousand notes
Of melodies on wings,
And enthralls me
With the great mystery
Of the immensity above
And what there is beyond.
Then He prepares me
With the tender sight
Of the autumn leaves,
And the mighty anger
Of the winter winds
And with its frosty breath
Caresses my lips.

My friend is called "Nature"
But I know His name...
God, the Almighty One.

MY VERY OWN

As I recall the days of yonder
When you were all much younger
And all the days were blue
And all I had was you
My very own to love
And as the world went on and on
With rains and snows and storms
We waited for the spring
Which brought green and everything
The birds brought songs
And the flowers bloomed
And so did you who loved me
My very own
And life was like a feast
And so was our world for all to see
And as you thrived like the willows
On a river bank
Our Lord I thanked
Feeling the joy of having you
For my very own
Our Lord I thanked

ALMOST A PRAYER

If you ever wonder
Why my words
In prose and in verse
Have been written and read

Try to empty your soul
of all bitterness,
By pouring it out
Onto paper or space,
When you are alone and tired
And there is nothing else.

Then what else could there be?
...The Grace of the Lord within me.

ANOTHER THOUGHT

High above the majestic pines on the front
lawn
Where the birds play and hum their songs,
I looked up to heaven as I have always done
With a morning prayer on my thoughts.

And there it was, a great expanse of blue,
serene and deep,
Waiting for my eyes and soul to feast.
Was it a pool? A lake? A sea?
With waves of silvery lace around its rim,
…Shrouded clouds in dark gray veils
moved billowing with the wind,
Turning my blue pool into a darken mist
Causing scattered tears to fall upon my feet.

A PRAYER

Dear Lord:
Give me some inspiration
And show me how
To tell the world
The happiness I feel,
The faith abundant
You have given me,
The blessings and the love
Which I received.
Thanking Thee, Oh Lord!
Is not enough to deserve Thee.
I need you Lord, now, within me
And the out of me,
So that the world may see
How true and great
The power of your Spirit is.

A THOUGHT OF YOU

Autumn is here with the scent
of soft and fruitful days;
And a hope of spring
just a thought away.

But first the warming gathering
of winter season,
Togetherness of body and soul
with quite a reason.

To praise, to sing,
to worship and adore
The greatest One who loves us all.
Forevermore.

PART II

REMINISCING

In my one hundred years of living, I have accumulated many sad thoughts of the past but also many happy memories of my long life. One of my favorite happy recollections is the one that I have put in my poem, "Loving Little Giants."

Long ago after years of working very hard, I bought a modest two-family Brownstone building in Brooklyn. It was in this high-ceiling old home with its creaking staircase and squeaking floorboards, where my beloved grandchildren grew up. Long after, the myriad of sounds that I remembered took wing, turning the audible patter of little feet into the big sounds of life and love.

A MOMENT UNGUARDED:

WHILE AWAY FROM HOME

Today a tear I shed
And tasted its salt
A moment of sadness
Enfolded my thoughts
Searching as always I am
In a forgotten purse
An old set of keys
Were found by my hand
I fingered the keys tenderly
And looking up yonder
I entered a door in wonder
A large handsome door
Of my old loving home.

Home! What a saintly word
A place where love remains
Pure and guiltless and with the grace
Of those who once in there dwelt

I looked at the walls
And at the hangings
And all which composed
The life and spirit of the home
My lips tightened with a grin
Like a smile not with pleasure
But of longings and wants for the love
And the joys forever enclosed
In the walls of my home.

I came back to the present serenity
Which life has bestowed upon me
And to the sweet solitude of my life
With God as my trust and belief
But as long as life is endured
And the mind is vivid with thought
I will long for the home of my years
Where all my darlings were born

But I know that though we are all scattered
Upon all the worldly winds
With a vivid link, our hearts
Shackled remain
'Till death us do part.

CHEERS

Cheers, cheers! Why not?
I have lived a great number of years
Happy? Perhaps not so,
But contentment has crept along
Making a life as daring as a game.

'Played with destiny and won
And if at the end of same
I have no boot to count
There is no one to blame-

But laughs and cheers
Will ease the tenseness of the years
That is left for father time
To win its game with life.

HOPE

When you are alone and away
From the one who is love
And the night is upon you
Without sleep
Let your want be a wish
Reaching beyond
Stirring the calm of the sea
Touching the heart of the one,
The beloved afar,
And so you will know
That a message of love
Was received and returned
And with a smile on your lips
You will soon fall asleep
Again and again.

LOVING YOU

A letter dedicated to my children and grandchildren

I often think of you my dear ones
More often than you would perceive
And of all the ties that bind us all
And all the years that passed so swift.

Years in which love grew for each other
tightly bound
Unforgotten years of togetherness to cherish
and adore
Years to treasure and tenderly recount
Years in which the thought of parting was
ignored.

Those tender years are past but not
dissolved
They are written down in mind and heart
To bring them out as time and age recall
And with a smile make sorrows part.

If there were struggles and toil all along
During those years alive in memories
The things you did that made me love you so
Are the things that made happiness for me.

No matter what old age may bring
The thought of you all in Almighty's hands
Have made dreams come true for me
While abiding in this our blessed land.

What does it matter if distance and crucial
times
Stand between us like unfriendly ghosts?
When the bridge of love is standing high
Waiting for...returning home.

As time goes on and no matter where you
stay
Look up with hope at the bridges of love
And never let your eyes go astray
For faith and light comes from above.

You are so vividly ingrained in my own being
That thinking of you is like a prayer and a
wish
And I think of you so often as to be
Like a morning light brightening the mist.

Like the need for nourishing like sleeping or
breathing
I need to think of you for living too.
There is no other purpose for existing
But for the thought of loving you.

And, don't ever forget
That love which dwells in the heart
Is like a treasure of diamonds and gold
Which no one can rob or despoil
And remains in the chest 'till you are old.

LOVING LITTLE GIANTS

As I recall the dearest echoes of noises past
And of a shaking stairway creaking
When running fast,
…Of loving little giants,
To say, "Good morning, Grand."
How Can I forget all that?
Their loving voices,
Their shuffling noises
Their "Hello, Grandmama."

My loving little giants
Today are gone.
In other places
Their voices tone.
And like sweet embraces
Their echoes dear
Are still at home.

THOUGHTS FROM SANTA'S "LITTLE GIANTS"...

The "creaking stairway" always gave us away. Even though I tried to tip-toe to her side while she was feverishly sewing a new dress on her noisy factory machine, she always knew when we were coming... always ready to lovingly greet us.

> Virginia Santa
> First Grandchild

...and my three sisters, such finely tuned little giants they have become. Be so proud.

> (Luisito) Jorge Jr.
> Third Grandchild – the "Prince"

The Fourth "Little Giant"

I was blessed to grow up with extended family near me at all times. Although it was difficult growing up without a father in the home, my Grandmother, Aunt and other close relatives offered the nurturing support and guidance that a growing child needs, especially with all the potential dangers and temptations of growing up in place like New York City. For me, my Grandmother was my foundation. Quite literally too, as we lived in a three-story brownstone with my grandmother living on the first floor, and my mother, three siblings and myself living in the floors above her. My grandmother has always been a source of strength for our family, and always lived her life as an example to others. She has been the most important role model in my life. She has always been there when someone needed her, always loving, always giving, hard working, self-motivated, intelligent, ingenuitive, creative, an outside of the box thinker, always a good friend to all, and let's not forget the best cook ever! I have often wondered how and why God has given our family such a wonderful and dear soul to share our lives with. Simply put, she is an angel. She is the angel God sent down from heaven to us to look after us all.

God Bless you, Abuelita.

> Margaret Montalvo Trunk
> Fourth Grandchild of Santos Pi

NO MORE SNOW

Ah, the sight of the new spring
The renewal of the self
And of every living thing
Though expected every year
It is always a wonder to me

In my solitary moments
Through my window glass I see
The new sprouting branches with its leaves
Bowing at the gentle breath of wind
Festooned and laced with satin blue
Embroidered around their edges green
Birds choreographing in and out the trees
Singing their own melodies
To the dancing leaves
Breaking the monotony of my winter dreams.

ONE LITTLE CHAPTER

Fifteen years away and I came back
We met again and quietly reminisced our past
He handsome still, eager and gay
I, a little shy but willing to play

Dinner for two and a band playing
He offered me a drink I did not accept
Cigarette?, he asked, opening a pack
I have not learn to smoke yet, I said
And now it is too late to start

He smiled a little and happily invited me to
dance
And I thought, perhaps to break the gap
Of all the years past
And then I said, I have forgotten even that

He smiled again and quietly sat
Dinner was served and I thought, perhaps
He being so happy and I so sad
No love can bloom with such a cast
And then he said, I found the one at last,
No drink, no smoke, no dance

My love, do not go back! Stay and be forever
mine
I smiled and looked into his eyes
It can never be again like that
We found and lost each other once (again).

POEM FROM MY SOUL

Lonely are the nights
When tender memories
Come from the past

Lonely are the moments
When you really wish
The impossible wish to go back

Painful and lonely are the hours
When you bring to the present
Memories that bruise your heart

And if your heart has grown
Hard and cold, untouched
By tender human hands
With a piercing painful shrill
Your heart will fall
And break in half.

SERENITY: WINTER

On warm winter mornings
I sit on my green front lawn
Where the birds coming from the north
Clasp their wings and hum their song,
And the morning grace
With its golden arms
Brightens my days
And gladdens my heart,
While murmuring breezes
Softly caress the jasmine frond
Dispersing its scented breath
Like a blessing touch upon my earth.

TALKING TO MY HEART

Oh! Quiet, quiet my heart,
Why do you pound so fast?
Has my passive but busy life
Given you cause to be so might?

While you are pounding so very fast
I bring to mind my quiet past.
Do not scare my life away,
It has been sad yet full of hope and faith.

Go easy, please, I am telling you.
At least, let me live my life in peace.
What have I done that in your wrath
You beat and beat without a flash.

Is it because in yonder days
No love would come your way
And only dreams that faith beheld
Made short the years that came and went.

Or is it because my busy life
Was lived in haste without a smile,
And by and by I went along
Without even a little song
To cheer you up or slow you down.

Oh! Heart of mine if I had known
What'd have made you tick without a groan...

THE LOVER OF MY YEARS

In the Spring on mornings clear
On my windowsill I sit
Waiting for the lover of my years
And quietly he comes unseen
Ah, the tender Zephyr,
That refreshing morning air
That caresses my face
And caresses my hair
And caresses my lips
With its tender tip of wings;
While my eyes, my soul.
On the quiet grandeur
Of God's creation I feast
If I could still the moment so dear
And forget the passing eras and all my tears

Then the radiant morning grace
On the horizon blue
Shows up his smiling face
And with his luscious hues
Brightens up the greens;
The lover of my years fades away
I close my window and sit and dream.

THE PROMISED HOUR

When the hands of time
Forever marks the promised hour
On the sphere of my heart,
And the infinite envelops me
In its eternal veil of mist,
And eternity holds my soul
In its finger tips
Where the spirits of the earth
Joins the spirits of the mist,
I will then float with grace
In the ethereal sea.
What greater felicity
Is there to desire and to reach?
I ask myself as I solitary sit.

THESE ARE THE DAYS

These are the days, my friends
"The days of wine and roses", someone said.
No, my friends, they were wrong.
These are the days of wine and mums,
The flowers blooming in late fall
When there is no more hope
Or trust, faith or belief.

In warm caressing fingers
Of a gentle wind
To touch the heart of the late buds
Of seeds that were planted long ago,

These are the days, my friends
To bloom before the winter comes
And open our colorful petals
To an oblivious world
And hope for a smile, a care, a thought.

THE WELL KEPT LAWN

At night the neighbor's windows, bright behind
the trees
With their back ground lights
Adorn the green canopy of lacy leaves
With an embroidered pattern of delight

I stand and look, my room in shadow
Ecstasy involves me in the gracious sight
It is as beautiful during the days
As it is during the nights

Even when the heavenly lights can not be
sighted
When the sky is in mourning plight
The windows of my friends are always lighted
To brighten up my nights

Noontime, the lights of heaven midway
Above the canopy of greens, my lawn will
shade
Early evening when the sun begins to fade
Shades of red, orange and blue
Fills with wondrous lights, the space
To make my happiness come true.

WHITE ROSAL (rosal is a rose bush)

I planted a white rosal
For my friend
Who shook my hand
And for those
Who tear my heart apart
I also planted a white rosal.

LONELY LIFE

Mine has been a lonely life
To travel through
All my years
But only you, Love, keep me going

Mine has been a lonely life
To travel through
All my years
Knowing that you, Love, are always close
Make less tears fall during the nights

This morning I sat quietly as I always do
To bring to mind, all the thoughts of you
To bring to mind the memories
That enriches my lonely life.

PART III

RECORDANDO

Estos versos estan dedicados
A todos aquellos que añoran
Su querida patria y sus raices

ANHELOS

¡Ay! Cómo recuerdo mi tranquila playa
Que a través de las décadas no he podido
olvidar
Ni del mar Caribe sus templadas aguas,
Ni la brisa que ondula el arroyo que corre
hacia el mar.

¡Ay! Cómo anhelo caminar por las veredas
Donde cuando niña abandonadamente recorrí
Probando grosellas, tamarindos y cerezas,
Escuchando la canción de mi coquí.

¡Ay! Cómo sueño con volver, ¡Deveras!
Aunque sea un momento, un instante nada más
Y contemplar en la noche su luna y sus
estrellas,
Aunque la distancia me vuelva a separar.

¡Ay! Cómo veo a través de mis ojos velados por
los años
A mi amado terruño que cambiado está,
Aunque el mar Caribe permanece aun cálido
Y aun la brisa ondula el arroyo que corre hacia
el mar;

¡Ay! Ya no quedan las tranquilas veredas
Donde cuando niña abandonadamente recorrí
Ya no quedan grosellas, tamarindos ni cerezas
Y solo queda llorando el coquí.

¡Ay! Yo también he cambiado con los años
Qué pasando en lejano y frío ambiente van,
Pero amor y anhelo por mi patria suelo,
Eso no, no cambiará.

1946

INOLVIDABLE

Te amé con cariño extraño
Cuando volví a verte de nuevo
Y al ver tus lindos contornos
Creí que estaba en el cielo.

En contemplación sublime
De tu belleza sin par
Me pareció comparar
Tu faz con la gloria eterna.

"Dichosos los que se van"
Dijo una vez, no se quien.
Yo digo, dichosos los que están
Siempre unidos a tus pies.

Los que dejaron tus playas
Hace algunos años ya
Sueñan con volver de nuevo
Y tus arenas besar.

Los que como yo no pueden
La tierra extraña dejar
Siempre sueñan con tus brisas
Tu playas y tu palmar.

Cuando yo dejé tu suelo
Era tu futura vida incierta.
Hoy sobresales del mar
Como una perla perfecta,

Encrustada en esmeraldas
Como una joya ducal
Bella, rica y reluciente
Sobre el terciopelo azul del mar.

!Oh, Islita! Todos te adoran.
Unos allá con amor, otros acá con desvelo.
Que Dios bendiga la tierra
Donde mecieron el coy de mis abuelos.

1944

MI PUEBLECITO, LA PLAYA

Cuantas veces a través de los años
Te he sostenido en mi mente
Cual te vi por última vez
Cubierto de sol resplandeciente
Tus verdes campiñas llenas de flores
Recorrí con mi alma sonriente
Entonces llena de tiernos amores
Mis labios tus frutas campestres probaron
Tus riachuelos mis pies refrescaron
Por tus veredas caminé llena de esperanzas
Sin temores vagué en tus noches veladas
En mis paseos admiré el misterio de tu luna
plateada

Cuando niña en las arenas de tu playa jugué
Y ya crecida bajo el sol
Un día mi nombre grabado dejé
Junto al nombre del amado de mi corazón
Pensé un día volver a pisar
Los caminos que me vieron sonriente
Y admirar la belleza de tus campos verdes
Y aunque ya sin esperanzas
Y el alma sin tiernos amores
Ya no hubo paseos bajo la luna plateada
Por tantos temores.

Y al ver de nuevo a mi playa
Donde cuando niña jugué
Y mi nombre grabado en la arena
Junto al de mi amado, un día dejé
¡Ay! dije, ya todo ha pasado
E intemamente lloré
Ya apenas existe la belleza
De ese pueblecito donde nací yo
Solo quedan estos versos llenos de congojas
Al verlo convertido en pavimento y sol.

1947

TIERRA MÍA

Yo quisiera decirte que sonrío
Que mi vida no es otra cosa que un edén
Que en mi existencia no hay nunca desvario
Que todo ha sido felicidad y placer

Que mientras vivo la esperanza me acompaña
Y cuando sueño es solo contigo
Y cada día que despierto en la mañana
Es falsedad lo soñado y mentira lo vivido.

No puedo decirte que muy pronto
Estaré a tu inolvidable lado
Pues los días no se hacen menos cortos
Ni los años menos largos.

Yo solo puedo cantarte, tierra mía
Y por eso dicen que hablo a solas
Y mi cantar son tristes poesías
Sublimadas en el alma que se inmola.

¿Cuantos años van que hablo conmigo?
Pretendiendo mitigar mi corazón
Que cansado de golpearse en sus latidos
Se detendrá algun día y con razón.

Y cuando en ésta tierra extraña y fría,
Inerte, mi cuerpo descanse a solas
Allá mi alma estará presente
En cada tumbar de las olas.

Brooklyn, N.Y. 1950

MI PUEBLITO

Cuando te abandoné por vez primera,
Pueblito de mis amores,
Triste, solitario y frágil eras
Pero cantaban tus ruiseñores.

Cuando niña y tu sol me acariciaba,
Jugué, formando castillos en las arenas de tu
playa
Mientras el aroma de jasmines
El ambiente perfumaba.
En tus noches no veladas,
Caminé por tus veredas
Llenas de luna plateada
Y envuelta en el perfume de tus flores
Iba mi alma entonces llena de tiernos amores.

¡Pueblito!, no eres cual otro,
Único en el eterno valle de mis sueños.
Pues aunque recorra el cosmo
Y visite las cercanías de otras playas
Y castillos en sus arenas haga,
Todo es inútil, solo mis castillos
Aún se elevan en las arenas ilusorias de tu playa

Porque solo tú vives aún en mi mundo
De memorias no olvidadas
No ha podido el calor de otro solado
Ni el tumulto de las trullas
Ni placeres disfrazados
Esfumar la imagen tuya.

No importa que yo he pasado
Cinco décadas lejos de ti, pueblito amado
En mi mente estás cual aquel día
Que me pareció dejarte abandonado.
Fuí en busca de un horizonte bello
Que vi tangible a los lejos
Y que aún yo no he alcanzado
Decadas frías, años febriles,
En el bello horizonte que había soñado

Solo encontré desconocidos cerriles
Retorcidos y solapados.
Y, como el ave, de volar cansada
Hoy añorando en pensamiento
El nido que una vez tuve en tu playa,
Quisiera volver, pues aunque próspera me
siento
Necesito el calor de tu seno y el abrigo de tus
alas.

Santos Pi Rivera
336 First St
Brooklyn, N.Y.
December 23, 1955

EL MAR

Un día yo pregunté, 'Mamá',
'¿Donde está la casa en que nací?'
¡Hija! El mal de mar se lo llevo todo.
'¿...El hogar donde nací?'
Y, veinte años después
También me ha llevado a mi.

Me llevó hasta extraños suelos
En busca de un nuevo hogar
Después de cuarenta inviernos
Al fin lo pude encontrar
Luchando con esas olas
Del mal del mar.

Ahora que al fin he triunfado
Contra ese mal del mar
Este hogar que yo he encontrado
Ya tu nunca lo veras
Yacis en silencio eterno
A las orillas del mar.

1956

CANTO A LA SOLEDAD

Eres emperatriz absoluta
Y abarcas nuestro mundo entero
Paredes, castillos en ruinas
Y ruinas humanas componen tu imperio.

No hay guerra que te limite
Ni paz que dominarte pueda
Es tu alma tan inmensa
Y tan duro tus confines
Que solo pueden vencerte
Angeles y querubines.

!Dominante! Que acaparas
Todo lo que al fin de la jornada se detiene
Yo te canto, porque te amo
Porque quisiera vencerte.

Las paredes y castillos de tus ruinas
Historias son, de glorias y riquezas idas
Y tus pobres ruinas humanas
Pilares que sostuvieron el mundo
Raices que alimentan la vida

Es tu abrazo corrosivo odiado tanto
Por agarrarse al corazón y marchitarlo
Y en tu perpetua, e incesante corrida
Destruyes almas, pisas vidas
En la agonía lenta de los años.

¡Ay! Soledad, a pesar de todo yo te canto
Porque gozo en tu presencia infinita
Y en tus confines me siento
Libre y dueña de mi propia vida.

1978

ARREPENTIDA

Por no apreciar el aroma
De la rosa que recibí un día
Deshojada quedó entre las páginas
Del libro que fué mi vida.

Sus pétalos desecados y marchitos
Son cada uno, una historia viva
De los años que pasaron lentos
Y hoy, al recordarlos en memorias mías
Cada pétalo de la rosa marchita y desecada
Fué una década vivida
Sin fragancia, prisionera y olvidada.

Al abrir hoy el libro que fué mi vida
Y contemplar la rosa que guardé un día
Solo espinas de su talle quedan
Que hieren por estar vivas.

1980

REFLEJOS

Mi espejo, el amigo de antaño
Que fuera tan fiel
Se ha vuelto adversario
Mostrando dobleces y zurcos
De los años flacos, los años de ayer.

Años que pasaron lentos
Con nieves furtivas
Y vientos traidores
Clamor de lamentos
Dolor y temores.

Mi juventud, única fortuna
Riqueza inalienable desde mi cuna.
Cuidé como joya preciosa
Con matices de arreboles
Herencia nativa de amor y de soles.

No fueron las nieves furtivas
Ni los años flacos y lentos
Que como ladrones de noche
Despojaron mi cofre
Desde mi aposento.

Fueron los vientos traidores
Aquietados anhelos, febriles antojos
Y ausencia de amores.
Y ya mis ojos añejos, velados
No alcanzan a ver lo trazado
Y pacientes se ocultan detrás de los párpados.

1983

CINCUENTA AÑOS DESPUÉS

Dedicado a mi amiga Julia Carmen Cruz

Ah, cuanto tiempo ha pasado sin creer
    En el cruel mudar de los años
    El espejo, mi amiga de antaño
    Que fuera tan fiel,
    En el cruel mudar de los años
    El espejo, mi amigo de antaño
    Se ha vuelto adversario
    Olvidando vestigios galanos de ayer
    Mostrando decadencias y ruinas
    De lo que ya fué.

Ah, Pasaron veloces los años
    Y dulzura se tornó en amargura,
    Y desamor y desvelos
    Movieron sus dedos
    Delineando en la fina textura
    Del semblante ufano
    Un mapa de surcos
    Con pliegues humanos.

Ah, envuelto en las sombras
    Parece el espejo
    Y sonríen los labios serenos
    Porque ya los ojos un poco velados
    No alcanzan a ver lo trazado
    Y tranquilos se ocultan
    Detrás de los párpados
    Y sueñan con lo ya vivido y lo ya soñado.

1983

ETERNA
Poema dedicada a Julia Torres
Pastora Emeritus, Playa Ponce

Aún recuerdo los pilares de mi pueblo.
Día tras día, todos desaparecieron
Dejando solo una torre
Que Dios dotó con un nombre
Desde su cuna, Julia Torres.

Pilar humano. Maestra divina,
Hoy te saludo, de Dios bendita.
Cuando marches al trono del cielo
Abandonando esta esfera,
Todo tu pueblo dirá como yo,
"Bendita seas!"

Tu nombre está escrito en el libro
Que arriba te espera.
La historia te debe una página
Y si la olvidaría, y no la escribiera,
Mi lira y mis versos tornado en campanas,
Táñiran eternamente tu nombre
Por todas las aulas.

El pintor halaga la vista,
El compositor festeja las ánimas
Pero tu arte humano y divino
Forjó mentes, corazónes y almas.
Cual otra no hubo dotado del cielo
Y por Dios inspirada.

Yo fuí fruto de tu arte divino y humano
Y hoy quisiera cantar con mi lira
Que forjó el "GRAN LIBRO" en tus manos,
Una sonata, sinfonía excelsa
Que lleve tu nombre; "JULIA TORRES".

Nueva York 1980

HORAS MUERTAS

Envueltas en velos de desesperanzas
Como fúnebre cortejo
Lentas y seguro avanzan
Conmigo las horas muertas

Añoranzas desenvueltas
De inquietudes ignoradas
Dejan sus huellas formadas
Durante las horas muertas

Desesperacíon profunda
Desgarradora por lenta
Llenan los intimos valles
De todas las horas muertas

Hay cuan frías las almas nuestras
Al fin de cada jornada
Esperando el velo eterno
Pasamos las horas muertas

El futuro ya no nos importa
El pasado apena ya se revela
Y aunque incompleta la historia
Avanzan las horas muertas

Horas muertas, horas muertas
Vacías, huecas, vanos, incompletas
Pausados, obstusas y lentas
De esos seres que ya ancianos
Solo tienen horas muertas.

EL CUENTECITO DE LA VIEJECITA Y SUS CUENTOS DE HADAS

Hace unos cuantos años ya, que en un pueblecito a la orilla del mar, vivía una viejecita amable y cariñosa que reunía todas las tardes al caer el sol, a los niños de sus vecinos para transportarlos a los rincones del mundo mas deseádos. Era como si Dios le hubiera dado el poder mágico de hacer los niños reir, soñar y sentirse felices, deseando ser héroes valientes y crear imperios.

Esa viejecita era pobre en bienes comunes, pero rica con el poder mágico de sus palabras que eran capaz de calmar las ansias de los niños, sus desvelos, dolor y hambre. Con sus palabras y paciencia, era capaz de conducir todos al cielo, cerca de la gloria, al fondo del mar a conocer las criaturas del oceáno y su bellaza acuática, a bosques poblados de animales juguetones, a jardines colmados de flores exóticas y perfumadas. Otras veces llevaba a los niños a la corte de reyes, donde se bailaba con música sublime que parecía ser escuchada por sus estáticos oídos. Otras noches los ninos eran invitados a banquetes imaginarios, plenos de sabrosos platos que aquietaban el hambre, como si verdaderamente hubieran disfrutado de la comida. Todo esto, en sus bellos cuentos y magnifica descripciones, el amor de la viejecita junto al esplendor de sus cuentos de hadas, tenían al gran poder de inspirar confianza y traer a la imaginación, la maravillosa creencia que todas esas cosas habían tomado lugar.

Los niños iban por el aire como pajaritos, pero siempre con plumajes de hermosos colores y nunca enjaulados, pues aunque algunos pajaritos durmieran en sus jaulas, los niños sabían por las palabras de la viejecita que inspiraban confianza, que las jaulas son necesarias también para descansar seguros y lejos de peligros.

Cada vez que los niños se reunían para es-cuchar a la viejecita, venían llenos de entu siasmo, deseosos de saber a donde irían esa no-che antes de dormir. El silencio dominaba en-tonces, en la salita pobre de la casa pequeñita, que en pocos momentos se convertía en salón elegante, o campiñas verdes o sitio de recreo donde todos se sentían felices. Los niños cerra-ban los ojos, fascinados al escuchar la voz dulce con su timbre acariciador, que hacía dormir y soñar. Cuando la viejecita se detenía un ins tante para renovar las fuerzas de su espíritu, los niños abrían los ojos, demandando más de la dulce voz, para continuar soñando.

Los cuentos de la viejecita eran adoradamente interminables. Ella endulzó con sus relatos la existencia de muchos niños, entre ellos, la mía y aunque yo era la menor entre todos, nunca me dormía y siempre escuchaba los cuentos hasta el fin.

La viejecita me bendecía todas las noches antes de irme a dormir. Ella era mi admirable mamá, mi adorada madrecita, y esos cuentos que escuché de sus labios cuando niña, los guardé entre los dobleces de mi cerebro, y hoy después de sesenta años, los he traido a la luz para dejarlos como herencia para todos aquellos que deseen disfrutar de mi tesoro. Mi tesoro, los cuentos de mi propia madrecita, que han sido mi única herencia, fueron como petalos de rosas esparcidos en mi paso por la vida, para enriquecerla con su belleza y fragancia. Recogí mi tesoro y lo guardé en mi memoria, como se guardan pétalos de rosas, momentos inolvidables, presados en libros, y quise extraerlos después de tantos años, y para conceder el honor a mi madrecita, he puesto los "Pétalos De Las Rosas De Mamá" aún vívidos y fragantes, entre las páginas de este libro.

La autora,
Santa (Santos) Pi